KINGDOM
THINKING

An Invitation to *Think* and *Live* the *Kingdom* Way

JOE JOE DAWSON

ISBN: 978-1-7350800-2-4

TABLE OF CONTENTS

CHAPTER 1

WHAT ARE YOU THINKING?

Have you ever felt stuck in life? Have you ever found yourself continually encountering the same issues time after time? Have you ever found yourself going around the same mountain over and over again caught in an endless cycle? If you have ever felt this way, it is most likely because you do not yet have Kingdom thinking. When our thinking is wrong, our decisions and circumstances will reflect it. I want to challenge every person reading this to confront the negative thought patterns that keep you from living your life to the fullest in God. A mind that is set on the Kingdom of God will manifest the Kingdom of God. So, let's start thinking Kingdom!

Over the years of life and in ministry, I can often sense what a person's thought life is probably like within the first three to five minutes of speaking with them. The way people speak and the words they use are strong indicators of what their thought life is like.

Unfortunately, if someone has negative thoughts, it is extremely obvious within the first few minutes of speaking with them. When I sense that someone may have wrong or negative thought patterns, I am not setting myself up as their judge. Instead, when I sense someone may have a wrong mindset, I am thinking of ways I can help them to shift it.

We've all encountered those that, unfortunately, have only negativity to share. Their words are negative, and their opinions are negative. So, each time we walk away from a conversation with them, we feel negative. However, we've also all encountered the kind of people that each time we see them are full of life, hope and always have something encouraging to say or something great to report.

What's the difference between the two? Well, you are a direct result of how you think about something and your life is directly tied to your thoughts. All our actions come from the belief systems we have established in our minds. If your thoughts are positive, your perspective will be positive. Even in difficult seasons or during tests and trials, a person with a renewed mind will come out on the other side stronger than before. However, a person who does not have Kingdom thinking will not be able to withstand difficulties or hard circumstances. The only difference is mindset, and the right mindset makes all the difference.

Positive thoughts will bring positive actions. Negative thoughts will bring negative actions. Positive people will attract other positive people into their lives. Negative people will always attract negative people into their lives. If you are struggling to determine what kind of mindset you have, look around at the results of your life. Are they positive or are they negative? If your life looks negative, it's probably because your thoughts were negative first.

If you take nothing else away from this book, remember this: Your life can only be as good as your mindset. Where your thoughts lead, your life will follow. So, what are you thinking? Proverbs 23:7 tells us, "For as a man thinks within himself, so is he." What Proverbs is telling us is that what we think is what we will become. This is why your thought life matters! If you will become what you think, is your mind fixed upon the right things? If your thoughts today became your reality tomorrow what would your life look like?

Each of our thoughts will eventually become actions and the way we react to situations can either make or break us! Every thought that we think matters more than we know. Our thoughts will eventually become our life. Whatever we think about, we will always bring about. You cannot outrun a negative mindset or reach your destiny with a defeated mentality. What consumes your mind will control your life, for better or for worse.

Unfortunately, I have seen many people who have immense potential never accomplish anything. Why? All because of a lack of Kingdom thinking. So, what is a thought life? What makes up a person's mindset? A mindset is an established set of attitudes held by someone. Our mindset is made up of all our thoughts, everything we believe to be true, and all of the learned patterns of thinking that we have carried with us our entire lives. This is why establishing a Kingdom thought life is so important for every believer!

Many talented and gifted people have fallen by the wayside of life because of their wrong thinking. Let this not be said of you, my friend! Romans 8:6-8 says, "The mind governed by the flesh is death, but the mind governed by the Spirit is life and peace. The mind governed by the flesh is hostile to God; it does not submit to God's law, nor can it do so. Those who are in the realm of the flesh cannot please God." If our mind is governed by the Spirit of God, we will be governed by the ways of His Kingdom. However, if our mind is governed by the flesh, our mind will be governed by the ways of this world. You cannot have Kingdom thinking and think negatively because there is no negativity in the Kingdom of God! Negative thoughts will produce a negative mindset every single time. And unfortunately, negative thoughts lead to negative actions. This is why many people find themselves trapped in an endless cycle of negativity that starts and ends with their mindset.

Have you ever faced a difficult season or circumstance and wondered, "How did I get here?" Well, unfortunately, the things we face and the circumstances we find ourselves in are often a result of something we have or haven't done. It all starts with our mindset. You are a direct result of what you think about yourself. Proverbs 23:7 says, "For as he thinks in his heart, so is he." Whatever you think about will be what you do and who you become. You can't have a negative mindset with a doom–and-gloom mentality and have a positive life or future. A negative mindset will always compete with a positive mindset. We must be diligent to tear down the strongholds that the devil has built in our minds over the years. Many of us believe the lies that the enemy has told us and those lies are destroying different areas of our lives.

So, if we want to change our lives, we must first change our thoughts. One of the hardest things you will ever change is your mind. Many people never step into their destiny or purpose because their mind has not been renewed. Romans 12:2 says, "And do not be conformed to this world, but be transformed by the renewing of your mind, that you may prove what is that good and acceptable and perfect will of God." There is power in having a renewed mind. I truly believe that many people miss the will of God for their lives because they have not taken the time to renew their mind in the Word and presence of God. To reach your purpose and destiny, your first step is to renew your mind. Allow the Lord to renew your mind by immersing and grounding yourself in the Word of God.

Psalm 119:9–11 says, "How can a young man cleanse his way? By taking heed according to your word. With my whole heart I have sought after you, O let me not wander from your commandments. Your word I have hidden in my heart, that I might not sin against you." The closer you draw to God every day, digging into His word, the harder it will be for you to fall away. Reading the Word daily and staying in prayer will keep the Lord's commandments before you. As long as you keep your mind freshly renewed in the Lord, it will always remain sharp and precise full of Kingdom thoughts. Ephesians 4:23–24 says, "Be renewed in the spirit of your mind, and that you put on the new man which was created according to God, and true righteousness and holiness." Kingdom thinking begins when we plant the seeds of God's word in our hearts and minds.

If we want everything that God has for us, we must have the thoughts of the Kingdom ruling in our minds. 2 Corinthians 10:4-5 says, "For the weapons of our warfare are not carnal but mighty in God for pulling down strongholds, casting down arguments and every high thing that exalts itself against the knowledge of God, bringing every thought into captivity to the obedience of Christ." We must be willing to confront wrong mindsets. If you don't believe that you are a true son or daughter of God, if you have a poverty mentality, if you think negatively about yourself and your life, confront those wrong mindsets. Our thoughts will not change unless we are willing to confront wrong thinking and bring every thought we have into obedience to the Word of God. Our thoughts should be a mirror reflection of what Heaven says about us.

As children of God, we are to have the mind of Christ about everything in our lives. A Kingdom thinker thinks differently than a person who is in the world. Why? Because as believers, we have access to the mind of Christ! Philippians 2:5 says, "Let this mind be in you which was also in Christ Jesus." Whenever I encounter a hard, difficult, or challenging situation, I will pray this Scripture. I pray to have the mind of Christ. I pray that I would see the situation the way that God sees it. I pray that I would think about the situation the way that the Lord does. I pray for my mindset and my perspective to be like God's. Why do I do this? Because I want to have the mind of Christ! I also want to respond and make decisions in a Christ-like manner. I want to have Kingdom thinking so that I can live a Kingdom life!

You see, my friend, the truth is if your thoughts are not Kingdom thoughts, you will not have a Kingdom mindset. As a believer, we must have a mindset made up of Kingdom thinking in order to do all that God has called each of us to do. Wrong thinking or a wrong mindset will keep you trapped in cycles, constantly delayed by roadblocks that will keep you from running after all that God has for you. However, there is hope! I believe that if you can correct your mindset and shift your thinking, nothing can stop you from reaching your full potential in God!

CHAPTER 2

STRONG-MINDED

Chuck Swindoll said, "I am convinced that life is 10% what happens to me and 90% how I react to it." This is why I want to share with you how to shift and strengthen your mind! If you can change your thoughts, you can change your life. Your thoughts will change how you react to even the worst situations or circumstances. When I become frustrated or upset with a person or a situation, I try my best not to respond or react. Instead, I ask the Holy Spirit to show me the Kingdom perspective and to give me the right mindset. The Lord is always faithful to show me His perspective of the person or the situation and because I can think about the situation from a Kingdom perspective, I am then able to respond the Kingdom way.

If we want a strong mind, we must learn to ignore our critics and any negative voice. Every one of us has a breathtaking purpose from God for our lives. I have seen too many people give up because one person spoke a negative word of criticism over their lives concerning the project they were working on. Whenever God elevates you to a higher level, you do not have to find your critics, they will find you. You must understand that critics are angry, jealous, and bitter because they are watching others do what they were called to do because they refused to step out in faith. Strong-minded believers have to identify the source of the criticism and then separate the person from the spirit fueling them. Make a conscious decision to forgive them in advance. The Lord Himself will ultimately step in to vindicate you, but in the meantime, you must keep your mind and heart free to continue to walk in God's love and power unhindered. A strong-minded person will always listen for God to speak before they seek anyone else's advice or opinion.

Strong-minded people react differently than those who are weak-minded. A person with a weak mindset can get a hangnail, and their entire day is ruined. On the other hand, a strong-minded person will encounter all kinds of difficulty and still keep going. When life comes against you, you must have Kingdom thinking. A person who has Kingdom thinking will look at any situation and know that they are an overcomer. A person with Kingdom thinking will determine in their mind that no matter what obstacle or hurdle they may come across; they will still keep moving forward with God.

Philippians 4:8-9 says, "So keep your thoughts continually fixed on all that is authentic and real, honorable and admirable, beautiful and respectful, pure and holy, merciful and kind. And fasten your thoughts on every glorious work of God, praising Him always. Follow the example of all that we have imparted to you and the God of peace will be with you in all things." We cannot have a negative, doom and gloom pattern of thinking and expect a positive future. We must put Philippians 4:8-9 into practice and fix our minds on the things of the Kingdom. When our minds are set on the Kingdom of God, we will find what is good, honorable and praise-worthy in everything, every person and every situation. Each time you interact with someone, you can choose to find the good or the bad in them. In every situation, you can choose to see the positive or the negative. In everything, you can choose to either what could go wrong or what could go right.

Our mindset is made up of choices that we make about our thinking. If we choose to always be negative, our mindset will continue to become more negative. However, if we choose to focus on those things that are admirable, good, just, and praiseworthy, then our mindset will become positive. Our mindset affects our choices, and our choices affect our mindset. Henry Ford says, "Whether you believe you can do a thing or not, you are right." If your mindset is that you can do anything in life, then you will be able to do anything. If your mindset is that you can't do anything in life, then you won't. A wrong mindset can derail your purpose and destiny.

The truth is whatever we think in our minds, our emotions, or our spirits is what we will become. We must be stable in our emotions, strong in our spirits and have the right mindsets in order to reach our destiny. So, a shift in your mindset is a powerful key to your destiny. 1 Samuel 30:6 says, "Now David was greatly distressed, for the people spoke of stoning him, because the soul of all the people was grieved, every man for his sons and his daughters. But David encouraged himself in the Lord his God." King David had every reason to be worried and distressed. Everyone around him wanted to kill him. But instead of giving in to his emotions or fear, David chose to strengthen and encourage himself in the Lord. Each morning, I stand in front of the mirror. I look at myself in the eye, and I say, "Joe Joe Dawson, you are going to have a great day. You are going to have a powerful day. You are going to move forward in every area of your life." I speak encouragement and life over myself. I do not look at my circumstances, the situation, or what anyone else has said about me. I declare what God has said about me over myself.

Each time you declare something, you are strengthening your mindset. This is true whether the declaration is positive or negative. If you declare that nothing good ever happens to you, this strengthens a negative mindset. But if you declare that God's goodness and favor chase you down, then you strengthen a positive mindset.

Isaiah 42:9 says, "Behold, the former things are come to pass, and new things do I declare: before they spring forth I tell you of them." The two words that I want to highlight in this passage are the words "former" and "declare." The word "former" has four basic one-word meanings: first, most, highest, and past. "Now the former things have come to pass." But here is what the word "former" means when it is broken down: the things that we think about first. It also means the things that we think about the most or give the highest regard and greatest priority. But what we must remember is that it refers to things of the past. When we think about our future, many times we tend to insert the former things, those things from our past. But unless you want history to constantly repeat itself, the former things are in the past and must firmly remain there. Now, the Lord is doing a new thing! So, quit allowing your mind to think on the former things first. Quit giving those things the greatest amount of thought and priority in your mind and quit putting them in the highest place. They are of the past and that is exactly where they need to stay—behind you!

Now the word I like the most in this Scripture is "declare," which simply means "to pronounce the something out loud." When you have to make a decision that will bring change, you have to be decisive about breaking from the past and moving forward into a new day. Will you go back to the former things and allow history to repeat itself, or will you stand up and declare that an opposite outcome will happen? You will not return to your past failures. You will not make the same mistakes again. You will not be silent any longer. You will no longer fall victim to the same recurring sin cycle. You are no longer insecure, etc. Declare your God-ordained future over your life. Stand up and pronounce that the opposite will happen and now is the time to move forward toward the things God has planned for you.

When I was a child, my dad always told people, "My boy can do that." Someone said, "No one can ride that bull," and my dad said, "Joe Joe can do that." So, at a very young age, even if something looked impossible, I was convinced that if my dad said I could do it, then I could. We must have that kind of thinking when it comes to the promises and prophetic words God has given us. Even if it looks like there is no way we can, we have the mindset that we can because God said we could.

My second-born daughter, Judah, is strong-minded and strong-willed. One summer, she created an exercise routine to stay in shape while she was out of school. She was explaining her routine to me, and I was impressed with how rigorous it was. Her routine included walking and running part of the time. So, she went outside, and I followed to watch her. Summertime in Texas is no joke. It was already very hot outside that morning. After just a few minutes of running, her face was flushed, and she was dripping with sweat, but she just kept going. She never once stopped to complain about how hot it was or how tired she was running in the heat. After several more minutes, the dad in me rose up, and I stopped her and asked, "Judah, it's pretty hot out here. How much longer are you going to do this?" She replied, "Just five more minutes" and took off running again. Judah did not stop until she had completed her scheduled exercise time. Strong-minded people ignore their feelings and their flesh in order to reach their goals.

Proverbs 4:23 says, "So above all, guard the affections of your heart, for they affect all that you are. Pay attention to the welfare of your innermost being, for from there flows the wellspring of life." This Scripture challenges us to guard our innermost being because the things of our lives spring from there. What is your innermost being? It's your thought life. Guard your faith and trust in God. My daughter, Judah, is one of the bravest and boldest people I have ever met. Why? Because she has developed a mindset that if I say she can do it, she can do it. Do you have that kind of confidence in God the Father? If not, when did you lose it? You must have the mindset that if God says you can, you can!

People who are spiritually and emotionally strong react to situations differently than those who are not. It's all about your mindset. Those who have spiritual and emotional stability are great stewards. Emotional and mental stability is so important. Your mindset can either lead you to success or to failure. Ask the Lord to prepare you and give you a strong mindset. Ask the Lord to establish you and stabilize your mind and emotions. 1 Corinthians 2:16 says that we have the mind of Christ. Tap into that and allow the Lord to give you His mindset. If you have a radical shift in your thinking, you will experience a radical shift in your life.

Strong-minded people are determined to keep going even when it is difficult, and they do not quit. To succeed in life, you need a strong mind and a finishing spirit. Successful people think differently from the average person. I learned a valuable lesson from my dad when I was very young. When my dad was young, he worked in a factory line. At one point, the management began letting many of the employees go. They were making budget cuts and laying people off. My dad, instead of having the mindset of a victim or giving into his circumstances, had a different mindset. He told me, "Son, my goal at work is to outwork the person beside me. I am going to outwork the man on my right and my left. I am going to make myself valuable to this company by outworking everyone around me." Because of this mindset, my dad never lost his job. My dad instilled this work ethic in me, which has made a huge difference in my life. If you have an average mindset, you will have an average work ethic. If you have an average work ethic, you will live an average life. Winners, champions, and successful people do what others are unwilling to do.

CHAPTER 3

MINDSET OR A SET MIND

There is a critical difference between a mindset and having a set mind. A mindset can either be positive or negative, an earthly mindset or a Kingdom mindset. However, a set mind is a mind that is made up. Every person needs to have a set of core beliefs that they cannot be talked out of. This is where having a set mind comes in. A set mind is a mind that will not be tossed to and fro by circumstances or situations, no matter what they are. A set mind is a mind that is not unstable or divided. A set mind is a mind rooted and grounded in the ways and principles of the Kingdom of God.

So, do you have a mindset or a set mind? What kind of mindset do you have? Do you find your mind filled with thoughts of doubt and fear? Or do you find yourself dreaming with God for the impossible? Bill Johnson, the senior leader and founder of Bethel Church, once said, "You know your mind is renewed when the impossible looks logical." When you see something impossible, do you think to yourself, "Yes, I can do that!" Or do you think, "There's no way I could ever do that?"

Mindset is what separates the best from the rest. When we have our mind set on moving forward in a certain area, we will let go of all the excuses. I once heard someone say, if you are looking for an excuse you will always find one. Is your mindset set on finding an excuse or do you have a mind that is set on moving forward?

As I've said before, a strong-minded person thinks differently than a weak-minded person. One of the characteristics of a strong-minded person is that when they set their minds on something, nothing can change it. Many never succeed or hit their mark in life simply because they give up or simply because they have not set their mind to push through and advance. If we find ourselves constantly stuck in the same areas of our lives over and over, it is time to get our mind set on the Kingdom of God. Don't stay caught in a negative mindset, instead become diligent to tear down the strongholds the devil has built up in your mind. 2 Corinthians 10:5 says, "Casting down arguments and every high thing that exalts itself against the knowledge of God, bringing every thought into captivity to the obedience of Christ." In order to have the right mindset, we must confront wrong mindsets. If our minds keep going to war over the same thing over and over, it's time to make that wrong mindset bow its knee to Jesus. Another translation of 2 Corinthians 10:5 says, "We can demolish every deceptive fantasy that opposes God and break through every arrogant attitude that is raised up in defiance of the true knowledge of God. We capture, like prisoners of war, every thought and insist that it bow in obedience to the Anointed One."

If you want to experience freedom in your thought life, you must allow the Word of God to transform your mind. John 14:6 says, "Jesus said to him, "I am the way, the truth, and the life. No one comes to the Father except through Me." John 1:1 says this about Jesus, "In the beginning was the Word, and the Word was with God, and the Word was God." John 8:31–32 says, "Then Jesus said to those Jews who believed Him, "If you abide in My word, you are My disciples indeed. And you shall know the truth, and the truth shall make you free." Jesus is the truth. He is the living Word of God, the ultimate truth, and that truth will be what sets us free. We will not be free in our mind until we plant the truth of God's Word and allow it to produce fruit in our mindset. The truth that Jesus is will break wrong mindsets.

When we spend time with the One who is the Word and who is the Truth, we will see our minds transformed. Matthew 6:6 says, "But you, when you pray, go into your room, and when you have shut your door, pray to your Father who is in the secret place; and your Father who sees in secret will reward you openly." This is why it is so important to spend time in the presence of God every single day. We encounter God in the secret place, and His truth sets us free. The more time you spend in the presence of God, the more your mindset will be transformed so that you have a Godly mindset.

In my daily pursuit of God, I am searching for one thing—Him. Psalm 27:4 tells us, "One thing have I desired of the Lord, that will I seek after; that I may dwell in the house of the Lord all the days of my life, to behold the beauty of the Lord, and to inquire in his temple". As I pursue Him, God reveals more of His destiny for me. I seek God more and more daily so I can know more about His personality and characteristics. When I do this, He responds by telling me more about who I am and all that I'm called to do.

Pursuing God is an amazing and fun journey, a journey that will change everything about you, including your mindset. One reason for this is because no one has ever experienced the complete fullness of God. God is never-ending and amazing, so I can have daily encounters with the Lord that are more powerful than any revival service. Philippians 3:12 says, "I admit that I haven't yet acquired the absolute fullness that I'm pursuing, but I run with passion into His abundance so that I may reach the destiny that Jesus Christ has called me to fulfill and wants me to discover."

When your life is completely surrendered and hidden in the Lord, your daily pursuit is to seek Him for who He is. In these moments, He speaks to our hearts and transforms everything. Our daily time with God shifts our thoughts and renews our minds, and then we begin to think the way God thinks. Set your mind on the Kingdom of God and allow the Lord to establish His Kingdom in your mindset.

Many of you reading this may be believing for breakthrough in your life. You may be believing for God to break through in many different areas and bring change and transformation. The truth is your breakthrough will come once your mindset has been transformed. I want to share this passage of Scripture with you. In 2 Samuel 5:20 David is going up to battle, and Scripture tells us that he went straight to Baal-Perazim and "He smashed his enemies to pieces." Afterward, David said, "God has exploded my enemies like a gush of water. Then David named that place, 'the Master who explodes.'" Another translation says, "David named this place, 'the Lord of the Breakthrough.'"

I want to encourage you today that the God of David is the same God today, and He is on your side for breakthrough—breakthrough in your mindset and breakthrough in your life! God is ready to take you from the place of wrong mindset that has kept you constricted, unable to move forward, and bring you out into a land of victory. God is ready to bring you out into a land of breakthrough!

Many times, when we are waiting for breakthrough, we can feel tempted to quit or give up. However, if you will set your mind, develop Kingdom thinking and stay the course you will reach your breakthrough. Just keep moving forward, don't give up and remain faithful as you wait, and God will come through for you! Every season is not about launching into something brand new. Some seasons are for simply staying the course. God answers our faithfulness and obedience with His power every time.

Build what God has placed in your hands. God will expand those that will set their mind and endure the process. Stay in the Word of God and stay in the place of prayer and you will get to your destiny. Keep your relationship with the Lord strong and listen for His voice. He will keep you focused on where you are going and in His perfect timing you will reach your appointed purpose and destiny!

Make up your mind now that you will stay the course and finish every season well. Keep your mind focused on the Lord and on what He has promised you. He will do every single thing He has promised you He would do. You may be praying for a prodigal son or daughter to come home. Keep praying and stay the course. You may be believing for financial breakthrough. Keep sowing seed, being a good steward and stay the course. You may be waiting for a miracle for you or a loved one, just keep believing! When God delivered the children of Israel out of Egypt, He did not lead them into the wilderness just to leave them there. God always brings us out of one thing, to lead us into something else. Don't take the wilderness for granted, but also, don't stay there. Get your mind set on the Kingdom and there is nothing you cannot do!

CHAPTER 4

THE WAR IN YOUR MIND

The war of your life is fought in your mind. This is why we must know what the Word of God says about how to fight. Ephesians 6:10 says, "Now finally, my beloved ones, be supernaturally infused with strength through your life-union with the Lord Jesus. Stand victorious with the force of His explosive power flowing in and through you". You must understand that you have to take a stand for what God has placed in your heart. God is asking every one of us not to budge an inch when it comes to the truth of His Word. God does an extreme work in us in our private prayer times and in our secret place of devotion. Then when we go out in public, He can flow freely and powerfully through us. God made us to be supernaturally filled with divine power when we call upon the name of Jesus. That explosive power can be used and manifested when you declare the will of God over somebody's life or in a particular situation.

Start thinking higher! Stand up and fight for complete victory in your mind. You have the power to call people's lives, situations, and circumstances into proper alignment. Ephesians 6:12 says, "Your hand-to-hand combat is not with human beings, but with the highest principalities and authorities operating in rebellion under the heavenly realms. For they are a powerful class of demon-gods and evil spirits that hold this dark world in bondage." We must realize we are not battling against flesh and blood in the fight over our minds, but we are battling against the enemy. In order to have victory in our minds, we must know that the enemy has already been defeated. 1 John 4:4 says, "You are of God, little children, and have overcome them, because He who is in you is greater than he who is in the world." No attack or scheme of the enemy that comes against us, not even in our minds, can overcome us because the God that is in us is greater than the enemy outside us.

Almost every situation and circumstance in life seems to have a faith or fear option. Many times, in life, we are faced with decisions. We must choose whether or not we are going to operate out of faith or fear. Far too many times, people choose fear over faith, especially when God is trying to change certain aspects of their lives. We must operate out of the faith realm, fully believing that God will be faithful to do everything He said He would do. 2 Timothy 1:7 says, "For God has not given us a spirit of fear, but of power and of love and of a sound mind." So, if fear is present in our lives and God does not give us fear, then who did? If there is fear in your life, where did it come from? I guarantee you it came straight from the enemy and it started as a seed of fear and doubt that he planted in your mind. Send it back. Return to sender! There is no fear in the Kingdom of God, therefore there is no place for fear in the thoughts of a Kingdom minded believer! Remember, your life will model which Kingdom you really live in! If you are walking in fear, the Kingdom of Darkness is ruling your thoughts. If you are walking in faith, then you are truly operating from the Kingdom of God!

Faith means having complete trust and confidence in God. On the other hand, fear means experiencing unpleasant emotions or anxiety over the outcome of something or fearing danger to someone. Whenever you or a family member receives a bad report from the doctor, do you insert faith or fear into the equation? When you receive a bad report about your job, do you deposit faith or fear into your own heart? If you have a prodigal son or daughter who should have been home hours ago, do not allow yourself to meditate on fearful thoughts. Rather, choose to pull on the faith in you and remind God of His promise that your child would serve Him and fulfill the mighty call on his or her life. Then rest easy, knowing the power of the Holy Spirit will draw him or her back.

Ephesians 1:18 says, "The eyes of your understanding being enlightened; that you may know what is the hope of His calling, what are the riches of the glory of His inheritance in the saints." We need to be enlightened so that we can understand how much is available to us in Christ. If we could see deeply into the spirit realm, we would understand that more is available to us than anybody can fathom or than has even been tapped into. The Lord has a powerful inheritance for His children. Many people fail to walk in this inheritance because they simply refuse to identify with the authority and power God has given us. The inheritance that God has for His children consists of many things: peace, grace, mercy, health, joy, prosperity, etc. The list goes on and on.

When we exercise our faith, we can see everything that we come in contact within every atmosphere completely change for the glory of God. The atmosphere at home in our families can be completely shifted by God's power. Our work environment can be changed because of our faith. Our financial situations can experience the limitless power of God. If we have a neighbor or family member who is sick, God's power is more than able to bring about healing. Everything about our day-to-day lives can be changed, and the power of God is made available to us to do so. However, it all starts with shifting our thinking to align with the Word and Kingdom of God. Ephesians 1:19 says, "My prayer for you is that every moment you will experience the measureless power of God made available to you through faith. Then your lives will be an advertisement of the immense power as it works through you." The apostle Paul is saying here that his earnest prayer and heart is that we will learn to experience the limitless power available to us as children of God.

Ephesians 1:20 goes on to say, "This is the explosive and mighty resurrection power that was released when God raised Christ from the dead and exalted him to the place of highest honor and supreme authority in the heavenly realm". The same mighty and explosive power that God Himself used to raise Jesus Christ from the dead is available to us. God used this power to raise Jesus up and place Him at His right hand in the highest place of honor. This means when you speak life over a person or situation, you call it forth all the way up until it is in its rightful place in Christ. When we stand in the authority of God and declare a thing, we put it in its rightful place. After His resurrection, Jesus's rightful place was not in the tomb any longer. It was at the right hand of the Father. You need to call some things out of the tomb. Begin to do so today. Be bold in declaring the manifestation of miracles with this mighty power. Command situations and circumstances to get into alignment with the Word of God.

We must remember Luke 10:19, where Jesus said to His disciples, "Behold, I give you power!" God has given us authority—His authority—which is delegated power. In the days ahead, greater waves of perversion will be coming to America. More strategic tricks of the enemy will be coming at us, so we need to be ready as children of God. Now when I said that, did you respond in faith or fear? We are about to walk into many years of the most powerful signs, wonders, and miracles the world has ever seen. Since masses of people are hurting and broken, we need a great revival of signs, wonders, and miracles. Because of the enormity and seriousness of the need, we are about to enter into an unprecedented season of explosive healing, deliverance, and restoration ministry with a central focus on the life-transforming message of the gospel of Jesus Christ. We need to have extreme faith because our assignments will require that we walk in high levels of authority and power from God.

Remember what Jesus said in John 14:12–14. "Most assuredly, I say to you, he who believes in me, the works that I do he will do also; and greater works than these he will do, because I go to my Father. And whatever you ask in my name, that I will do, that the Father may be glorified in the Son. If you ask anything in my name, I will do it." One day, the disciples were probably talking to Jesus about the messages He was preaching and the miraculous signs and wonders He was performing. They were likely reminiscing about all the devils He cast out in the regions He visited and about all the awesome wonders they had witnessed.

Then Jesus said something like, "Guys, you think all that is cool? You think what I do is awesome? I am about to go be at the right hand of the Father, and when He sends the Holy Spirit, you will do the same things that you have seen Me do. In fact, I love you so much that I am going to let you, as the new body of Christ, do greater works than I have ever done." For the body of Christ to do greater works than Jesus did, we'd better be ready to walk in signs, wonders, and miracles with extreme authority. When the Holy Spirit moves us toward a certain situation or person, we must operate in extreme faith to see the outcome that God intended.

Matthew 18:18, "Assuredly, I say to you, whatever you bind on earth will be bound in heaven, and whatever you loose on earth will be loosed in heaven." Look at the Scripture this way: If someone comes to you bound or handcuffed by the enemy, you simply pray for them and declare freedom over their life. The handcuffs open, and they are completely freed from whatever was binding them. Then they are loosed. Now as certain as that person is loosed from what used to bind them, you take the handcuffs and bind the devil in that situation over that person's life. Where they were bound, they are now free. Where the enemy had control, now he has none in that situation over them. We have that power when we call upon the name of the Lord and pray, especially when we earnestly intercede on behalf of others from a place of Christlike love, genuine compassion, and purity of heart.

Matthew 18:19–20 tells us, "Again, I say to you that if two of you agree on earth concerning anything that they ask, it will be done for them by My Father in heaven. For where two or three are gathered together in My name, I am there in the midst of them." Remember, whenever a few of us get together to pray, the mighty, miracle-working power of the Holy Spirit is right there in the midst of us. So, pray with confidence, knowing that God has your back.

In the natural, the body is made up of many different parts, but the head controls the body. The same is true in the spiritual realm. Jesus Christ is the head and we, the church, are His body. Where the head tells us to go, we go; when we go, we go in power. God has so much stored up for His people. He needs the body of Christ to be complete and made whole, so we do not limp or stagger into battle every day. Rather through Christ, we go in with hearts and minds full of the promises of God. In this frame of mind, we are ready to impact all our surroundings and transform every atmosphere that we walk into with the presence of God. We have the power to do that, you know!

Ephesians 3:19 says, "To know the love of Christ which passes knowledge; that you may be filled with all the fullness of God." We must each experience the love and power of Christ for ourselves. It is not enough to just read about it and think you truly know it. It is so much more than just head knowledge. God wants us to be completely filled and flooded with all of His fullness. You are supposed to live a life of overflowing love, joy, peace, favor, increase, and blessings. I want all that God has for me spiritually, physically, emotionally, financially, and mentally; and I want the same for you!

Ephesians 3:20 says, "Now to Him who is able to do exceedingly abundantly above all that we ask or think, according to the power that works in us." When we truly tap into the Kingdom of God and understand how it operates, we will have Kingdom thinking. Then we will have exceedingly, abundantly, above all that we can ask for in the place of prayer! With this kind of elevated thinking we will have more than we can even think about. It is all according to the authority and power level that we have working inside us. When you think with God's mindset, this Scripture makes complete sense. You do not pray for yourself personally to be blessed with earthly things as the main point of focus in your walk with God. You focus rather on the things of the Kingdom and strongly desire that God would use you to help orchestrate His divine plan for the earth. When we think like the Kingdom, we begin to live the Kingdom way!

CHAPTER 5

SUPERNATURAL THINKING

There are many believers who think naturally instead of thinking supernaturally. This is not the Kingdom way of thinking! God needs His people to be strong in their minds and spirits. We cannot give in to fear, anxiety, or insecurities when the enemy brings them our way. We must stay focused on the Lord and the words He has spoken over our lives. In order to have supernatural thinking, we cannot be double-minded.

A mindset dominated by natural thinking is a fleshly mindset and will always compete with a spirit-led or renewed mindset. An earthly focused mindset will always be at war with a Kingdom mindset. James 1:8 says, "A double-minded man is unstable in all his ways." Far too many times, I have seen people who receive an impartation from God and are running strong after the Lord and what He has for them suddenly fall off course because they were double-minded. The Word says that these kinds of people are double-minded and unstable in all their ways. These people are very scary and toxic individuals to associate with because you will start to depend and rely on them, but as soon as an attack comes, they completely bail out of the project they were co-laboring with you on. This is because many people have not developed a strong and steadfast mind in Christ.

This is why Colossians 3:2–3 says, "Set your mind on things above, not on things on the earth. For you died, and your life is hidden with Christ in God." You are seated with Jesus in heavenly places, and you need to keep your mind set on that reality. Don't be distracted or discouraged by what is going on in the natural. Your thoughts must stay focused on the Kingdom of God and what God has called you to do. All that a person achieves and accomplishes or fails to achieve or accomplish is a direct result of his or her thought life. We each have seeds of destiny, leadership, and greatness inside of us, but the problem is some of us are trying to figure it all out in the natural!

When God gives you a supernatural word, you can't figure it out in the natural. God is calling His people to live from a heavenly reality. To operate in heavenly reality, our mindset must be right. We must have the mind of God about whatever He has spoken to us. The Lord once spoke to this to me, "Don't try to figure out every season you go through. Nothing will make sense in the natural. But if you will listen to Me, I will guide, lead, and strengthen you by My spirit. But don't try to figure it all out." This is where many people miss it. They will try to make sense of supernatural things in the natural instead of following the leading of the Lord.

Colossians 3:2, "Yes, feast on all of the treasures of the heavenly realm and fill your thoughts with heavenly realities." Nothing in the earth can truly satisfy us. We must feast on the things of heaven. The reality of heaven is that God has an amazing, life-altering plan for you. But He needs to plant it in you so He can work it through you to see it manifested on the earth. Dreams, purpose, and callings come from heavenly reality. The giftings and the grace God has placed on our lives come from there as well.

Colossians 3:2 goes on to say, "Do not be distracted in this natural realm". When God speaks to you about a heavenly reality over your life, He already has a vision and a plan for it. But you have to cooperate with God to bring it to pass in the earth. When God calls you to do something, it is already a heavenly reality, and you just have to say yes. Let me use an example. If God calls you to step out and launch a business, you might start listing off what you don't have in order to do that. You might say, "I don't have a building or an LLC. I don't have my paperwork filled out. I don't have this, and I don't have that." But you don't need any of that yet. You have everything you need in order to move forward. You have a word from God! All you need to do is say yes and step out on His word. When you step out on His word, He will make sure everything else works out. When you get a hold of this heavenly reality, you will move in a Kingdom mindset. Don't let the distractions of this world keep you from walking in a heavenly reality. If you let the natural things distract you, you will never accomplish what God has called you to.

To operate in a heavenly reality, our thinking must be different. To operate supernaturally, we must think supernaturally. Romans 12:2 says, "Stop imitating the ideas and the opinions of the culture around you but be inwardly transformed by the Holy Spirit through a total reformation of how you think." When you receive a fresh download from Heaven you cannot operate in it in the natural. You cannot take a supernatural, spiritual word and try to fit it into the ideas and opinions of the natural realm. Romans 8:5–8 states, "Those who are motivated by the flesh only pursue what benefits themselves but those who live by the impulses of the Holy Spirit are motivated by pure spiritual realities. For the mindset of the flesh is dead and the mindset controlled by the Spirit finds life & peace." I don't know about you, but I want peace. I want the mindset of the Holy Spirit. I want the Holy Spirit to guide, lead, and move me. I don't want my thinking to be weighed down by the limitations of this natural realm. This is why I cannot live with a mindset of the flesh. I don't want to live my life just from this earthly realm with earthly thinking. I want my life to reflect the Kingdom of God so my thoughts must first be rooted in the supernatural. This verse goes on to say, "The mindset of the flesh actually fights God's plan and refuses to submit to His directions. For now, no matter how hard they try, God finds no pleasure in those who are controlled by the flesh." I have seen more people with God-ideas fail, because once they start to go after it, they get too caught up in the natural. I've seen people stop following the Holy Spirit and go after the ways of the flesh. God is not pleased by this. We must be directed by the guiding and the leading of the Holy Spirit.

My wife, Autumn says this, "The whole world may know who you are, except for you." In our many years of life and ministry, we have encountered many passionate and talented believers that lacked one thing, a true understanding of their identity in God. To truly think the Kingdom way, we must first know which Kingdom we belong to! When you have changed the way, you think about your identity, your entire mind will change. This is why before Jesus had done any miracles or started his earthly ministry, the Father made sure Jesus knew exactly what the Father had to say about Him.

Matthew 3:16-17 "When He had been baptized, Jesus came up immediately from the water; and behold, the Heavens were opened to Him, and He saw the Spirit of God descending like a dove and alighting upon Him. And suddenly a voice came from Heaven, saying, "This is My beloved Son, in whom I am well pleased." What a powerful example of the affirmation of the Father toward Jesus, His Son! This was the confirmation that God spoke to Jesus. God called Jesus not just His son, but His beloved Son. God says the exact same thing about you. You are not just His son or daughter. You are His beloved son or daughter and you are important to God and His Kingdom. This is why the enemy wants to battle you over your identity in your mind, because there is power in knowing your identity!

We are not the only ones that have to fight this war in our minds over our identity. The devil immediately began questioning Jesus' identity when He had been affirmed by the Father. Matthew 4:1-3 says, "Then Jesus was led up by the Spirit into the wilderness to be tempted by the devil. And when He had fasted forty days and forty nights, afterward He was hungry. Now when the devil came to Him, he said, "If You are the Son of God, command that these stones become bread."

The very first thing that the devil did was try to get Jesus to question His identity as the Son of God. He questioned Him by saying, "If you are the Son of God…?" The devil was questioning His identity.

Did Jesus not already hear that from His Father? Whenever we hear affirmation from God, we must realize that the enemy will try to come in and steal our sense of identity and security in Christ. This is why a mind dominated by Kingdom thoughts is so critical. If we are unsure of our identity, then we will believe the enemy's lies. The enemy wants us to feel unworthy of what God has said about us and unworthy to do what God has called us to do.

The next thing the enemy said was, "Turn these stones into bread." The enemy said this to try to get Jesus' mind off of what He was called to do and get Him to focus on carnal things. The enemy could not get Jesus to question His identity, so he tried to get Him to compromise. When you know who you are in Christ, the enemy will always try to make you compromise. The devil will try to whisper confusion into our ears in an attempt to distract us because he knows if he can win the battle in your mind, he can win the battle of your life. The enemy will use many of these things to try to pull us away from thinking Kingdom. When we are not seeking the Father, spending intimate time with Him on a regular basis, it is easier for the enemy to attack our minds and try to get us to question our identity.

Matthew 4:4 says, "But Jesus answered and said, "It is written, 'Man shall not live by bread alone, but by every word that proceeds from the mouth of God." Jesus answered the devil right back with the Word of God. God wants us to follow Jesus' example in dealing with the devil and his lies and temptations. Jesus knew that if he kept the enemy's lies out of His mindset, then He could overcome any obstacle. Whenever the devil comes questioning our identity, we can overcome every single attempt with the Word of God, just like Jesus.

The most powerful thing you have in your natural body is your mind. If the enemy can control the way you think, he can control everything about you. This is why we must keep a current and fresh personal relationship with Jesus Christ and our minds continually renewed by the Word of God. Daily time with God will empower you to have Kingdom thinking that will overcome any wrong mindset! Mark 4:24 tells us, "Then He said to them, 'Take heed what you hear. With the same measure you use, it will be measured to you; and to you who hear, more will be given.'" Your mindset must be in line with the written Word of God and the prophetic words over your life. When those two types of words align with your God-given gifts and talents, there is nothing that can stop you from thinking and living the Kingdom way.

CHAPTER 6

DEVELOP WELL

Jim Rohn says this, "You can have more because you can become more—and unless you change how you are, you will always have what you've got." Do you want more? Do you want a closer walk with God? Do you want to prosper financially? If we want more, we must become more. One of the principles I live my life by is to always stretch myself beyond my comfort zone.

When I first launched into the housing business that my father-in-law and I have together, I bought the second rent house before I owned the first one. Then I started buying two at a time. Now, at the time I am writing this, all of the houses we rent are turning a profit.

When I first started filming videos, I would only film a couple of videos at a time. Now, at the time I am writing this, I can shoot up to 20 videos in one day.

Why? Because I intentionally stretched myself each time our film team came in to shoot the videos. Every time we filmed; I would push myself a little more. In what areas do you need to become more so that you can have more? Push yourself outside of your comfort zone, put forth more effort to become more so that you can have the more that God has for you!

Myles Munroe once said, "Nothing truly changes until your mind changes." I don't care how much excitement or zeal you may have for God. Until you change your mindset, nothing will truly change. 1 Peter 1:13 says, "So then, prepare your hearts and minds for action! Stay alert and fix your hope firmly on the marvelous grace that is coming to you. For when Jesus Christ is unveiled, a greater measure of grace will be released to you." Do you know what action means? It means to get up and do something! Action is a verb. This Scripture is prompting us to take action and allow the Lord to change our minds. When you take action and start moving toward your God-given dreams and destiny, the grace and anointing on your life will immediately increase. If you want to see change, take action and start with your thinking!

The human mind can be like a garden, if it is well tended it will produce amazing fruit! However, if it is overtaken by the lies of the enemy or by negative thought patterns, the fruit God wants it to produce will be choked out. You will grow what you plant. If you don't tend to the garden of your mind you will get unwanted weeds. If you carefully tend the garden of your mind there is no measure to the fruit God will produce through your life!

An undeveloped mindset will lead you astray on your journey to your purpose and destiny. However, the good news is that when we spend time renewing our mind and developing a healthy thought life, our situation begins to change. When we intentionally develop our thinking, we will begin to see success and begin to thrive. "Thrive" means "to grow or develop vigorously" or well; "to grow vigorously, to prosper, to progress toward or reach a goal." On the other hand, "survival" is "the state or fact of continuing to live or exist, typically in spite of an accident, ordeal, or difficult circumstances." The Bible is filled with the importance of thriving. Psalm 92:12 says, "Look how you've made all your lovers to flourish like palm trees, each one growing in victory, standing with strength!" Proverbs 11:28 says, "The righteous will thrive like a green leaf." God created you to thrive not just to survive. Many people go through life just trying to get by. You were never meant to live that way. God wants you to win in life, and it all starts with a mindset to thrive. If you are weak in any other areas of life, you must learn to develop those areas.

Earl Nightingale said, "One hour per day of study in your chosen field is all it takes. One hour per day of study will put you at the top of your field within three years. Within five years you'll be a national authority. In seven years, you can be one of the best people in the world at what you do." When I was first being identified by some Apostolic voices that I trusted in my life as an Apostle, I didn't really know what an Apostle was or how they functioned. So, I started buying and reading as many books as I could about the Apostolic gifting and grace that I could. I was reading and listening to as much content on the Apostolic as I could find. In another season, when I began a housing business with my father-in-law I began to read and study business books. I found two men in my city that were successful in that business already and asked them for advice and guidance. Why? Because if God was calling me to something, I wanted to do it with everything within me. If I am going to invest my time and energy doing something, I want to become an expert in my field. This is what I call a growth mindset. A person with a growth mindset never wants to do anything half-way. A growth mindset will motivate you to always be learning and growing in anything and everything that God has called them to do.

Earl Nightingale was talking about a job or a trade, but I want to talk to you about your walk with God and the gifts He has placed inside you. What if you read and prayed for one hour every day? What would your life look like one year from now if you set aside one hour to develop what God has placed inside you?

People who are greatly used by God set themselves apart to develop their relationship with the Lord and their gifting because they want to be used by God. The generals and giants in the faith that we look up to had a mindset to develop what God had given them so that they could do great things for the Kingdom of God.

In order to be successful and to thrive in every area of our lives, we must start each day with intention. A great place to start is to begin each day with God. Mark 1:35 tells us Jesus rose early each morning and went away to be alone with His Father. If it was important to Jesus, it should be important to us. Seeking the Kingdom of God first will help us live in obedience to Him. It will keep our minds on the thoughts of God instead of our own, and we will see transformation. Psalm 119:15 says, "I will meditate on Your precepts, and keep my eyes on Your ways." If you meditate on the concepts of the Kingdom, seeking the Kingdom of God first, then you will function out of a right mindset.

Philippians 3:14 says, "I press toward the goal for the prize of the upward call of God in Christ Jesus." Our prize is the upward call of God in Christ Jesus. The word "upward" in this passage refers to a heavenly calling. God has placed an upward call on every one of our lives. Through a close personal and intimate relationship with Him, we will find our God-given destiny.

We have to press in towards the Lord daily by seeking His face and getting to know Him more. The closer we are to the Lord, the more we will know about ourselves because our true life is hidden in Christ. When you have a daily relationship with the Lord, pressing toward the mark He has for you will become easy. Your mindset will change; you will begin to thrive and know what you are aiming for. Think about it this way: If you are shooting a gun but you are not aiming toward a mark, you will miss the goal. If you and your family left for a vacation without a final destination, you would be traveling aimlessly. My friend, as we draw close to God daily, we become closer to our destiny as we aim at the mark God desires us to hit. Every day, we press toward the goal that God has set before us by daily walking with Him.

Vision is one of the most powerful tools God has given us to help renew and transform the way we think. Proverbs 29:18 says, "When there is no revelation, people cast off restraint." Another translation says, "Where there is no clear prophetic vision, people quickly wander astray". The Bible clearly tells us that vision isn't just important. Vision is what keeps us on track; it is what keeps us alive. Without any vision for your life, you will go astray and miss your mark. Without vision, your mind will be filled with all kinds of unprofitable things.

The happiest people have a vision for their future and what they are called to do. People without any vision live a life that is very loose: loose with time, energy, words, relationships, work, and everything else. In Genesis 49:3–4, Israel is talking to his firstborn son Reuben, and he says, "Son, I love you. But you're like water! You conform to whatever and whoever you are around!" Why was Reuben so loose with his living? Why was he as unstable as water? It was because he had no vision for his life.

When you have vision for your life, you will value the purpose God has given you. You will think differently about what you do, who you are around, and who you want to become. Your destiny won't let you go everywhere, and your purpose won't let you hang out with everyone. If you surround yourself with people who have no vision, you will end up vision-less. If you surround yourself with people who are full of vision, you will be inspired and motivated to keep moving forward with whatever vision God has given you.

Many years ago, when I first started to work out, I was skinny as a rail. But I found myself working out with men that were just as skinny as I was. Then, I saw a group of men that I call "the swole patrol." These guys were very fit and very strong. I began working out with them because I had a vision of what I wanted my fitness to look like. When I first got married, I found several men who I thought had successful marriages, and I took each of them to lunch separately and asked them to teach me how to be a great husband and how to have a successful marriage. I did the same thing when we first had children. I found couples who were successful parents and asked them to teach me how they parented their children that behaved so well. It is important to find people who can speak into the vision God has given you for your life and glean from their wisdom.

I encourage you today, my friend, get vision. Meditating on God's vision for your life will change everything about the way you think. Get the vision that God has for your life and always keep it before you. Go after it and don't live loosely. Live with a purpose and determination to always move forward into your destiny and everything that God has for you. When you allow the Lord to develop your mindset you will begin to thrive in life and as you thrive God will give you more of the vision He has for your life. Never stop growing in your mindset and God will never stop growing you!

CHAPTER 7

KEEP GROWING

Luke 6:45 says, "For the overflow of what has been stored in your heart will be seen by your fruit and will be heard in your words." The way you think will dictate what kind of fruit your life produces. It will also reflect in the words you speak. Every thought we think has the ability to become like a seed in our minds that can produce Godly or ungodly fruit in our lives. If we want to change the type of fruit we produce, then we need to look at what kind of seeds we are planting. What kind of seeds are you planting?

All throughout the Bible, God gives us revelation using parables and stories. He often does this by mainly relating spiritual ideas to natural ideas. We see many similarities between how things happen in the natural and how things operate in the spirit. I once came across an article about five reasons why seeds do not grow in the natural. It reminded me of Matthew 13:1–9 which says, "On the same day Jesus went out of the house and sat by the sea. And great multitudes were gathered together to Him, so that He got into a boat and sat; and the whole multitude stood on the shore. Then He spoke many things to them in parables, saying: "Behold, a sower went out to sow. And as he sowed, some seed fell by the wayside; and the birds came and devoured them. Some fell on stony places, where they did not have much earth; and they immediately sprang up because they had no depth of earth. But when the sun was up they were scorched, and because they had no root they withered away. And some fell among thorns, and the thorns sprang up and choked them. But others fell on good ground and yielded a crop: some a hundredfold, some sixty, some thirty. He who has ears to hear, let him hear!"

We don't see fruit or growth in our lives from the seed God has planted for some of the same reasons in both the natural and the spiritual. Many of the same hindrances occur in the spirit with spiritual seeds. We will receive from the wisdom and the understanding of God through these.

The first reason that seeds do not grow is because they are planted too deep. Many people over complicate their spirituality and become too deep to reproduce. Developing a Kingdom thought life is so important. Don't allow wrong thinking to hinder you from growing. Many times, we allow other people to push us down and throw dirt on us by speaking negatively over our lives. If a seed is planted too deep, it takes too long to reach the surface, and the seed dies. We cannot allow others to throw things on us that will choke out the seed God has planted within us. The loudest voice in our lives should always be the Holy Spirit. Many people are so close to their breakthrough. But in order to break through to the surface and begin to grow, you must separate yourself from people who are constantly pushing you down. Negative people will try to keep you down because they know when you breakthrough, the favor of God will hit you. They do not want you to grow because they refuse to grow.

The second reason that seeds don't grow is because they are planted in bad soil. Most of you are good seed and some of you are even great seed, but you might be planted in bad soil. The problem is no matter how great of a seed you are, if you are planted in bad soil, you will never have what you need in order to grow. You can be surrounded by the most wonderful people in the world, but if you have a negative thought pattern, your seed will not grow. The same is true if you have Kingdom thinking but are surrounded by negative and toxic people. I have seen so many talented people with powerful callings, but they are planted in bad soil. Therefore, they will never get the nutrients they need in order to grow. This is why I like to equip, train, and encourage anyone God connects to Autumn and I to go and do all that God has called them to do! A lot of you are just in the wrong kind of environment. You are good seed! And when good seed is planted in good soil, a good harvest comes forth. But good seed in bad soil will never grow. If you are not growing, you've got to leave. You are too valuable to God, so you must plant yourself in a ministry that will help you grow. You are too important to the Kingdom of God to allow a lack of Kingdom thinking to hinder your growth. You must plant yourself around people who are not insecure or intimidated by you. You are not called to just go to church; you are called to grow the church.

The third reason seeds do not grow is because of weather conditions. If the environment you are in is not the right temperature, you will not grow. You cannot stay in an ice-cold church if you are burning for God. You cannot grow under a pastor or a leader that has no prayer life. If the leadership of the church you are in refuses to come to a prayer meeting, you are wasting your time. Too many people are good seed, but they are hanging on in frozen dead churches. They will give of their time and spend many hours in intercession for the cold church. I've heard many people use the excuse that God has them still at a dead church because they are called to pray for revival in that church. But I am here to tell you, my friend, if you are not the head, you are wasting your time. Many of you are good seed, and you feel discouraged because you have been faithfully praying, but you're praying into bad soil. You're praying into soil that has poor weather conditions that cannot support growth. Another way weather conditions can affect growth is if it is the wrong season. The Lord is walking some of you through a winter season, and you're trying to blossom. In order to see growth, you must be in the right place at the right time doing the right thing. Wait for the right season.

The fourth reason seeds do not grow is because birds and animals come in and steal the seed. You may be running with people who are after your seed. Don't put your seed around people who do not value it. Some people will want to steal your seed because they do not have their own harvest. You need to remove toxic people and those who only want to take from you from your life. They are only there to try to steal your seed. Proverbs 27:17 says, "Iron sharpens iron and a man sharpens the countenance of his friends." The Bible does not say that one always pours out and the other takes all the time. That is called an unbalanced, unhealthy relationship. Any healthy relationship requires give and take. You must surround yourself with people that are not seed snatchers.

The fifth reason seeds cannot grow is because the gardener or caretakers do not tend to it daily. You must have a daily consistent walk with God. You also need to surround yourself with those that are willing to intercede for you daily. You must make sure you are planted in a place where people will pray for you daily.

Think about it in the natural. If you do not water a plant for several days, it will start to wilt. You need to find good friends who will help water the seed God has placed inside you. Friends help friends grow. Some of you are not growing because your pastor or your apostle has given you everything they possibly can, and it is time for you to go. This is why, as an apostle, I must grow every day of my life so that the people aligned with me can always grow. Pastors and apostles must always stay fresh and current with God so that they can grow and help the people around them keep growing.

Ultimately, seeds do not grow when they are limited by their container and environment. If we are limited in our minds, our ability to produce fruit will be limited. But when there is no limit and no measure put on a seed, it can always keep growing and producing. Always make sure that you are stewarding your mind in a way that cultivates growth and freedom for the Holy Spirit to move your mind and your life every day.

Every apple seed has a tree inside it. Each seed has the potential to produce countless fruit. Your frame of mind must be to see the apples inside of the apple seed. When others see only apples, see the potential for orchards. Look at the people around you and call out their potential even when they are in seed form. John 12:24 says, "Most assuredly, I say to you, unless a grain of wheat falls into the ground and dies, it remains alone; but if it dies, it produces much grain." Some people stay in seed form with untapped potential because they never die to their flesh and open up in order to produce fruit. The reason many people are unsuccessful is not because they are void of potential but because they haven't been willing to plant themselves in the will of God. We must be willing to die to the flesh to produce fruit and multiply ourselves.

I want to encourage you that it is never too late to change your mindset and start producing fruit. Isaiah 54:1 says, "'Sing, O barren, you who have not borne! Break forth into singing, and cry aloud, you who have not labored with child! For more are the children of the desolate than the children of the married woman,' says the Lord. 'Enlarge the place of your tent, and let them stretch out the curtains of your dwellings; do not spare; lengthen your cords, and strengthen your stakes.'" Barrenness means not having fruit or not able to produce. Just because you may have been barren in the past does not mean the same will be true of your future.

Please understand that this passage means that when those who have long been barren finally begin to experience fruitfulness, they will have a higher ability to produce fruit faster than those who have been fruitful all along. If you've had a negative or a wrong mindset that has kept you barren, it is not too late for you! Allow the Lord to radically shift the way you think and watch the abundance of Kingdom fruit that comes forth from your life. Plant yourself by the river of God, get your mind rooted and grounded in the truth, and you will bear more fruit than you ever imagined. Psalms 1:3 says, "He shall be like a tree planted by the rivers of water, that brings forth its fruit in its season, whose leaf also shall not wither; and whatever he does shall prosper."

Ephesians 3:20 says, "Never doubt God's mighty power to work in you and accomplish all this. He will achieve infinitely more than your greatest request, your most unbelievable dream, and exceed your wildest imagination! He will outdo them all, for his miraculous power constantly energizes you." If you get the seed God has given you in the right environment, then you will see God do more in and through your life than you ever dreamed. The seed in you can change your life and your family. It can change your city, your region, and the world. That seed inside you needs to be nurtured so that it can grow and produce even more fruit. This is why you must protect it and tend to your mind as if it were actually the soil in the garden of your life. Cultivate your mindset, protect the seed God has given you, and watch your life explode with radical growth. If you can change the way you think, you can change your entire life.

CHAPTER 8

KINGDOM THINKING

There will always be so much more to say about thinking and living the Kingdom way. The ways of the Kingdom are so vast and supernatural that we could never fully comprehend them with our natural minds. This is why God wants to give us His mindset. If we truly want to see the Kingdom come in our lives, families, churches and in the world, it begins with allowing the Kingdom of God to invade our minds.

All of the promises and prophetic words that God has given you about your purpose and destiny are true! Every single one of the words God has spoken to you will come to pass when your mind is filled with the thoughts of the Kingdom. Godly thoughts produced by a renewed mind will keep you on the path God has for you, and you will hit your mark. But with the wrong mindset, you will be tossed back and forth by circumstances and what you see in the natural. Wrong thoughts will keep you distracted and delay your purpose. However, if we focus intensely on God and the calling, He has placed on our lives we won't let anything keep us from fulfilling every promise and assignment He has given to us. Proverbs 4:25 says, "Set your gaze on the path before you. With fixed purpose, looking straight ahead, ignore life's distractions." If we are constantly focusing on all of the things going on in the natural, we will be influenced by the world instead of the Kingdom. The world is overrun by fear and control. The Kingdom is ruled by the voice of God and His principles. Do not allow your thoughts to be swayed and influenced by the world. Allow the Lord to strengthen your mind so that you will not be distracted by whatever may come your way.

You will succeed in everything that you do if you will first commit it and your thoughts about it to God. Proverbs 16:3 says, "Before you do anything, put your trust totally in God and not in yourself. Then every plan you make will succeed." Another translation says, "Commit your works to the Lord, and your thoughts will be established". God will establish whatever you put your hands to if you will commit your thoughts and your work to Him. I love this Scripture in Proverbs because it promises that every plan we make will succeed when we surrender them and our thoughts to Him. You can be in the right place at the right time doing the exact right thing, but if your thoughts are not the thoughts of the Kingdom, you will never succeed. This is why we must allow the Lord to establish and direct our thoughts.

We must commit our thoughts and our work to the Lord every single day. Every day, I go into my time of prayer and recommit everything I'm working on, every thought I've had, and every part of me to the Lord. He has spoken to me many times in prayer and corrected how I thought about a person or a situation and kept me from becoming frustrated or offended. At times, I've been working on a project, and God will speak to me about a different way to do it. It turned out ten times better than it would have if He hadn't spoken to me about it. If you allow the Lord to establish your thoughts, then you will be able to commit your work to Him, and He will receive the glory from all of it.

The good news is, we are not alone on this journey of transforming the way we think. In Psalm 32:8-9, some of my favorite Scriptures, the Lord promises to always lead and guide us. Psalm 32:8-9 says, "I hear the Lord saying, "I will stay close to you, instructing and guiding you along the pathway for your life. I will advise you along the way and lead you forth with my eyes as your guide. So don't make it difficult; don't be stubborn when I take you where you've not been before. Don't make me tug you and pull you along. Just come with me!" Here God promises to lead and guide us on the pathway to our destiny, even if He has to drag us there! What we must understand is when we have Kingdom thinking, God will lead and guide us in the way we should go. When we trust in the Lord, our thoughts become like His thoughts and we will be sensitive to His leading. When our thoughts are Kingdom thoughts the Lord will never find us stubborn, having to be pulled along as He tries to get us where He wants us to go. The journey to our purpose and destiny can be breathtaking if we can learn to surrender our thinking and our ways in exchange for God's way of thinking and the ways of His Kingdom!

Allow the Holy Spirit to guide you. Nothing is more rewarding and fun in this life as living with your whole heart focused on God and what He has for you. What would your life be like if every aspect were pointed in the direction God intends for you to go? There would be no limit to the success God will bring in your direction.

John 16:13 says, "But when the truth-giving Spirit comes, he will unveil the reality of every truth within you. He won't speak his own message, but only what he hears from the Father, and he will reveal prophetically to you what is to come." Hang on to your prophetic words! God once showed me a prophetic vision of what it looks like to hold onto the prophetic words He has given to us. In the vision, I saw a lifesaver or a life preserver flotation device on the side of a boat. Then I heard the Lord say, "Do you know why I give people prophetic words? I give prophetic promises as a lifesaver to people when they are about to drown and feel as if they are sinking. My prophetic promises are like a lifesaver that people can hold onto when they feel as if they may go under."

When you feel as if you are sinking in life, hang onto the dreams, the promises, the prophetic words, and the purpose that God has given you. Hang onto them as if they were a lifesaver, because they are. You have to learn how to use your prophetic words as a flotation device. Many times, in life, if you only look through a natural lens at your circumstances, you will see that nothing is making sense. However, you can hang on to the prophetic words and promises when you feel as if you are sinking and going under. You will not go under or drown because the Holy Spirit will keep you afloat with lifesaving promises.

The prophetic words given to you by God are like a lifesaver because you can hang onto it. In the natural, if someone has gone overboard or is drowning, they will throw them a lifesaver flotation device. The person that needs to be rescued can hang on to the lifesaver, and the person on the other end can pull them to safety with the attached rope. You may feel as if you are sinking, but God has thrown you a prophetic word you can hang on to while you wait for the Holy Spirit to pull you back in close and into safety. You will not drown if you hang on to every word God has given you.

Many waste entire seasons of their lives treading water, spending all their time, energy, and effort to keep from going under. It does not have to be this way. Shift your thoughts and see your prophetic words and promises as a lifesaver and hang onto them! When you encounter seasons or situations when you feel as if you can barely keep your head above water, grab hold of the prophetic words God has given you. They will be a lifesaver to you. In your darkest moments, do not give up or let go. Hang onto every word that God has spoken to you because He is faithful to fulfill every promise. Make up your mind that you will not drown. Set your mind now that no matter how impossible your situation or how high the waters may seem; you will not go under or be overtaken. God will do everything that He has told you He will do, but your mindset will determine whether you sink or swim. Hang onto the Word and promises of God, and you will reach your destiny and destination! Let the ways of the Kingdom invade your thoughts and you will live and think the Kingdom way!

ABOUT THE AUTHOR

Joe Joe Dawson is the Founder and Apostle of Roar Apostolic Network and Roar Church Texarkana. Joe Joe is married to the love of his life, Autumn Dawson. Together they have three children Malachi, Judah, and Ezra. The Dawson's teach a lifestyle of revival and awakening. Their desire is to see every believer fulfill their God-given destiny and live life to the fullest in God. Joe Joe is the author of The 40 P's Of The Apostolic, Destiny Dimensions, and Living Your God-Sized Dream. He is also the host of Kingdom Mindset Podcast on the Charisma Podcast Network.

CONNECT WITH JOE JOE

JOE JOE DAWSON
FACEBOOK

@JOE_JOE_DAWSONTXK
INSTAGRAM

@PASTORJOEDAWSON
TWITTER

JOE JOE DAWSON
YOUTUBE

@JOEJOEDAWSON
PERISCOPE

JOEJOEDAWSON.NET
WEBSITE

The Kingdom Mindset podcast encourages, equips, trains, and motivates listeners to fulfill their purpose and destiny with a Kingdom mindset. Join host Joe Joe Dawson as he explores and dives into a wide range of topics that will transform and inspire you to become all that God has called you to be. Tune in every Monday at CharismaPodcastNetwork.com

Roar Apostolic Network is a network of believers who are contending for revival and awakening. Our heart is to help train and equip every person and ministry that comes into alignment with us. We are called to walk in the fullness of God's authority and power while abiding in the Father's love. Our calling is to help others reach their God-given dreams and destiny. This network is built for a church, ministry, pastor, business person, intercessor, believer, etc. ROAR stands for Revival, Outpouring, Awakening, and Reformation.

For more information, visit roarapostolicnetwork.com

All of Joe Joe Dawson's books have been administrated by McFarland Creative. McFarland Creative offers full book facilitation that includes book editing, interior design, formatting & cover design. We will take your vision for the book inside of you and make it a reality. If you are interested in sharing your words with the world, email info@mcfarland-creative.com today!